D1497997

E 88947

J 551.24

DATE DUE

READING POWER

Nature's Greatest Hits

Mauna Loa
World's Largest Active Volcano

Joanne Mattern

The Rosen Publishing Group's
PowerKids Press™
New York

Published in 2002 by The Rosen Publishing Group, Inc.
29 East 21st Street, New York, NY 10010

First Edition

Book Design: Michael DeLisio

Photo Credits: Cover, pp. 4–5 © Michael T. Sedam/Corbis; pp. 8–9, 13c © James L. Amos/Corbis; pp. 10–11, 18–19 © Viesti Collection; pp. 12–13 © Jim Sugar Photography/Corbis; p.13a © Morton Beebe, SF/Corbis; p. 13b © Corbis; pp. 14–15 © Richard A. Cooke/Corbis; pp. 16–17, 16 (inset) © Roger Ressmeyer/Corbis; pp. 20–21 © Peter Arnold

Mattern, Joanne, 1963–
Mauna Loa : world's largest active volcano / Joanne Mattern.
   p. cm. — (Nature's greatest hits)
Includes bibliographical references and index.
ISBN 0-8239-6014-5 (lib. bdg.)
1. Mauna Loa (Hawaii Island, Hawaii)—Juvenile literature. [1. Mauna Loa (Hawaii Island, Hawaii) 2. Volcanoes.] I. Title. II. Series.
QE523.M38 M36 2001
551.21'09969'1—dc21

                                            2001000602

Manufactured in the United States of America

Contents

World's Largest
    Active Volcano   4

Location   6

Size   8

Eruptions   12

Glossary   22

Resources   23

Index   24

Word Count   24

Note   24

World's Largest Active Volcano

Mauna Loa is the largest active volcano in the world. Mauna Loa is 56,000 feet tall. It's almost twice as tall as Mount Everest. That's more than ten and one-half miles high!

IT'S A FACT: *Mauna Loa* is Hawaiian for "long mountain."

Location

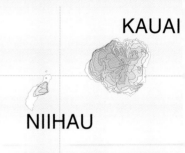

KAUAI

NIIHAU

Mauna Loa covers half of the largest island in the state of Hawaii. This big island is also called Hawaii. The Hawaiian Islands are in the Pacific Ocean. They are about 2,400 miles from the western coast of the United States.

IT'S A FACT: All of the Hawaiian Islands were formed by volcanoes.

OAHU

Honolulu ★

H A W A I I A N   I S L A N D S

MOLOKAI

LANAI

KAHOOLAWE

Haleakala Crater

MAUI

HAWAII

•Hilo

Mauna Loa Crater ▲   Kilauea Crater

*P a c i f i c
O c e a n*

California

Hawaii

Size

Only 13,680 feet of Mauna Loa are above sea level. The rest of the volcano is under the ocean.

Peak of Mauna Loa

13,680 feet

Sea Level

56,000 feet

42,320 feet

Base of Mauna Loa

Ocean Floor

When Mauna Loa is measured from its base on the ocean floor to its peak, it is the tallest mountain in the world.

All volcanoes have craters on top. The crater on Mauna Loa is four square miles. It is 500 to 600 feet deep. That's the length of two football fields.

Eruptions

Some scientists think that Mauna Loa first erupted as long as one million years ago. Mauna Loa's longest eruption lasted for 18 months in 1855 and 1856.

IT'S A FACT: Mauna Loa has erupted 15 times since 1900. That makes it one of the most active volcanoes on Earth.

Lava is melted rock that comes from inside the volcano. Hot lava comes out of the volcano when it erupts.

15

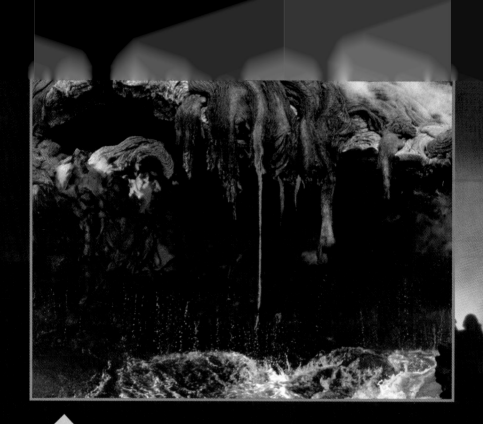

When lava reaches the ocean, it raises the water's temperature.

Lava is very hot. The temperature of lava can go as high as 2,000 degrees Fahrenheit. That's almost ten times as hot as boiling water.

Mauna Loa's last eruption was in 1984. The lava came close to the town of Hilo.

The lava was only four miles away.
Lava has destroyed some villages
around Mauna Loa.

Scientists are trying to understand what makes Mauna Loa erupt. People who live near the world's largest active volcano wonder when it will erupt again. Only time will tell.

Glossary

crater (**kray**-tuhr) the large opening at the top of a volcano

eruption (ih-**ruhp**-shuhn) when steam, ashes, and lava burst from a volcano

Fahrenheit (**far**-uhn-hyt) a way of measuring temperature with 32 degrees being the temperature at which water freezes

Hawaii (huh-**wy**-ee) the 50th state of the United States; also the biggest island of the Hawaiian Islands

lava (**lah**-vuh) the hot, melted rock that comes out of a volcano

sea level (**see lehv**-uhl) the point from which the height or depth of a place is measured

temperature (**tehm**-puhr-uh-chuhr) how hot or cold something is

volcano (vahl-**kay**-noh) an opening in the earth's crust through which steam, ashes, and lava sometimes are forced out

Resources

Books

DK Pockets: Volcanoes
by John Farndon
Dorling Kindersley Publishing (1998)

Volcanoes
by Seymour Simon
Mulberry Books (1995)

Web Site

United States Geological Survey:
    Hawaiian Volcano Observatory
http://hvo.wr.usgs.gov/maunaloa

Index

C
crater, 7, 10

E
eruption, 12, 18

H
Hawaii, 6–7
Hilo, 7, 18

L
lava, 14, 16, 18–19

M
Mount Everest, 4

P
Pacific Ocean, 6–7

S
sea level, 8–9

T
temperature, 16

V
volcano, 4, 6, 8, 10, 12, 14, 20

Word Count: 281

Note to Librarians, Teachers, and Parents

If reading is a challenge, Reading Power is a solution! Reading Power is perfect for readers who want high-interest subject matter at an accessible reading level. These fact-filled, photo-illustrated books are designed for readers who want straightforward vocabulary, engaging topics, and a manageable reading experience. With clear picture/text correspondence, leveled Reading Power books put the reader in charge. Now readers have the power to get the information they want and the skills they need in a user-friendly format.